Reflections
of the Soul

Charles Holmes

Reflections of the Soul

Copyright © 2018 Charles Holmes

Printed in the United States of America

Published by

Big Hat Press
Lafayette, California
www.bighatpress.com

_____

Cover Painting | Watercolor
"Great Blue Heron in Swamp"
Nancy Ricker Rhett

DEDICATED TO

Charles John Holmes, Sr.
and
Aidan Lee Elenteny

BOOKS BY CHARLES HOLMES

POETRY BOOKS

Streets That Speak*
For Understanding Eyes
Reflections of the Heart
Reflections of the Soul

*About streets that do not have enough and streets
that do have enough

NON-FICTION BOOKS

Hard Life, Kindness Ever Awake[†]
Thoughts From Millie**

**Interview quotes/practical wisdom from an elder
at 89, 90, and 91 years old

CHILDREN'S BOOKS

Bo Loney Goes to a New School
The Silver-lettered Poem in the Sky
The Cloth of 100 Wrinkles
Aidan Dreams Amazing Dreams
Aidan Dreams of 105 Fortune Cookies
Kid-like Poetry with a Bit of a Smile...Sometimes
Kid-like Poetry for Kids Who Are "Cool" at School
Kid-like Poetry for Kids Who Like Recess
Shy Kai Wished He Could Fly[†]

[†]In process

Available on Amazon
To contact author, please email rlg121212@gmail.com

CONTENTS

I

II

III

IV

PREAMBLE

I am a poet because my dear mother was a poet. I am a continuation of her heart. My words are her words. I was also moved to write these last few years by my love for my surrogate grandson, 10 year old Aidan.

My study formally and privately over many years has helped my efforts greatly, along with sufferings, hurdles, and substantial support.

I write to touch people's lives, that they in reading my work perhaps at times awaken a feeling, and gain a thought or two.

I

Courage I

So much life in the dark,
        beauty veiled,
grace under stone,
        courage in unknown souls.

No One Should Die Alone

If you should go before my time,
        I want to be at your side,
when your last breath dissolves in awaiting air.

Then I can push my cart in the street,
        solids to the market for coin,
thinking of you along the way,
        starting dialogue which will never end.

My remaining days going over lessons you taught,
        listen to your soothing voice
which strengthened and guided my steps,
        forever grateful for meeting on that spot,
where a secret shrine to build.

Every day is good,
        but without your star,
springtime to matter not,
        autumn leaves
mere scatterings on eyed pavement,
        daylight to be dark,
night time frozen, bottomless,
        no dawn miracle
to offer wonder to earthly mind.

Poems

Do poems inspire more feelings than stories,
      sensitive to uninterested eyes,
sense their potential,
      have concern about what is not understood;

tell enough about the hand behind the pen,
      experience joy when their eloquence peaks,
feel purpose on its way,
      words going deep, then deeper;

calm with those who choose not to read them,
      content having given all,
know the power of their art,
      realize they are music to the soul?

When a Mother Dies

It's a different world when a mother dies,
　　　more evidence of the power of love.
Intellectually, it can be a time for gratitude
　　　of what and who was given,
　　　and what and who was received,
emotionally, it's the beginning of dialogue beyond,
　　　an approach which only goes so far, but is essential.
Sometimes, the process must be let go,
　　　because loving so much causes too much pain.
But the dialogue is taken up again
　　　and mutual communication continues,
ever flowing, ever vital, ever necessary,
　　　tender mystical transmitting,
personal inner proof that life goes on.
　　　The cards read "Sympathy," "A Full Life,"
"Have gratitude,"
　　　but the profound message neither written
nor spoken is
　　　"Begin dialoguing."

Along the Way

Some walk over others
    trying to make a mark in their earthly stay.
Still, sacred road-sign reads:
    "It's the people you meet along the way."

Missing Out

We've all missed out,
      to accept, ignore,
don't wrestle with it,
      forget the loss,
focus on how to control the day,
      conscious of being in touch
with what matters.

Clouds

Clouds are not just up there,
      they are the landscape of the journey,
they learn how to fall, roll with, drift back,
      meet the steep mountain, pathless sky.

They enjoy rhythmic growth,
      strength to live through a storm,
descending, dispersing, hovering,
      sweeping down, swirling up.

They determine their mission,
      taking space made for them,
awakening high art, which sees
      the power of a spirit-filled atmosphere.

Their burdens are opportunities to expand,
      move forward even above moaning ocean,
saying to darkness there will be light,
      live rainbow on horizon near.

They attend to breathing and thrive,
      have a home within,
come together in their own special way,
      going about their day.

Unknown Souls

Faceless wanderers on country roads
        bestowing heartfelt glances,
guiding fingers, timely smiles
        at turning streams, mighty boulders,
high hills, open land, old farm
        houses nestled comfortably.

If only trails could speak,
        trees tell, flowers whisper, branches say,
great humanity, delicate and deep, would find a stage
to energize
        those who choose to walk in dark forest
        on sunny days.

When stepping amidst nature,
        titles fade in the wind,
shadows become jewels,
        majestic oak influences mind and spirit.

Birds sing above footway,
        some fly in cluster, others by themselves,
birds chirping a different tune,
        but knowing self
        and positive perception penetrating.
Graceful forgiving amid choking weeds
        which come through crowded pebbles,
path of peace to round-topped mountain,
        vision in the sun, valleys seen now as never before,
this time with appreciating eyes.

What is Core?

Love, says Camus,
     freedom, Dostoevsky,
serenity, Hesse,
     truth, Gandhi,
simplicity, Tolstoy.

Who is right?
     Perhaps Hesse's serenity,
visualizing Buber's
     "I and Thou."

Still, how academic
     in a world
which has yet to prove
     it cares.

Why Am I Here?

Why am I here?
to dance to music I cannot hear,
listen to silvery rhyme without valid reason,
play a greedy tune in favorable season,
dig a well and hope I thirst,
be a wandering monk who is not first,
Why am I here?

What is my passion,
majestic dome or rustic home,
clockwork or service-work,
patching pot holes or piecing together poetry,
using boxing glove or reverencing lifelong love,
being clogged and down-trodden, or
seeing that shadowy gate is open.
Why am I here?

What is my dogma,
precepts on scripture page,
clearer insights coming with age,
indolent stretching for golden rod,
hungry love awkwardly odd, or...
broken steps not allowed to worsen,
striving to become the best possible person,
broken steps not allowed to worsen,
striving to become the best possible person.

Wings

So much off center on planet of little caring,
       dollar's magnet, title's awe stretch generously,
inner child's soul feels pierce of countless dark arrows,
       elder's demeanor scarcely pleasing,
MANY OBSERVE, FEW SEE,
       MANY LISTEN, FEW HEAR,
more mirrors than eye glasses,
       more branches leaning low than springing out.

Though, birds sing after weather rage,
       breathe anew,
confident at water edge,
       calm in flight,
comfort on finding nest.

Freedom quest,
       mighty wings enabling,
Freedom quest,
       mighty wings enabling.

Why So?

Flowers on grave
     until children die,
then grassy dirt on tombstone,
     'til wind sweeps bare,
grandchildren rare.

II

Courage II

We are all such deep…
        unexplored territory.

May stranger within
        create steps of courage.

Baroness Traudl di Pauli

Gertrude (Traudl) is gone,
    loving soul
who cared more than most,
    Ghana's poor knows,
woman of action,
    prayer her daily way.
Her mother endured World War I & II,
    she, the latter,
along with her older sister, Barbara,
    who went before her.
She had great goodness in her veins,
    spent her generous humanity
trying to help the disadvantaged,
    last few years Parkinson's disease her fate.
Her spirit though, ever alive…still giving,
    Baroness Traudl di Pauli.

Meeting

Souls meet
>in sunny land of flowers,

core connection,
>mysterious and beautiful.

Conscious words
>only go so far;

little things
>count greatly.

Two humans bonding,
>work of living art.

It's the relationship,
>not necessarily the expression of it.

Living Goodness

Her mother died when she was 9,
        her father gone before.
Without parents, high school education,
        religious instruction, she lived nobly
untaught values.

Health-minded beyond her years,
        loved green tea, celery, parsley juice,
animals, about whom she said
        "don't hurt the way humans do."

No bad words about those mean to her,
        always optimistic,
clearly did the best she could,
        looked at the bright side,
consistently cheerful.

Saint in small studio
        on traffic-laden street,
cars rushing by, never noticing
        great soul behind curtained window.

Dorothy Day

1897-1980

We had lunch twice,
      1961, 1962.
She was obviously
      quite well-read,
would quote noted authors
      with ease, naturalness.
I asked what was most
      important in her life.
Her instant reply,
      her daughter.

Beauty From the Shore

Big wave
    with ineffable beauty,
flashing poetry with roaring sound,
    water magic fascinating,
delightful moment in the day.

Old Poetic Souls

Self-made none,
       helped in so many ways,
and they too often forgotten,
       ones who laid bricks,
so the house could have windows.

Now another season,
       New Beginning,
flowers to stretch in melting snow,
       petals to laugh at worldly wind.

"It's all for the best," said Dr. Pangloss,"*
       tho everyone's mosaic not memories of gold,
still great souls remind,
       don't waste this time.

*Voltaire's _Candide_

Why?

WHY didn't I know at 35
  what understanding eyes
could see later on?

WHY didn't I hold on to an idea
  long enough to associate it
with other thoughts more closely?

WHY haven't I done a
  a 5 minute SOUND meditation
before?

WHY did I put off
  reviewing the day's Little Joys
at evening-tide?

WHY do I focus on
  what I can't
control?

Poet and the Sea

Poet belongs by the sea,
        where else can he be,
perhaps near love
        or a tree.
Here I can be free
        to some degree,
sensitive to water,
        shore and sand.
Words come with water gaze;
        emotions touched in ocean roar.
If there's stress by the sea,
        it could be me.

Being There

Present to casual exchange,
   paths not to cross again,
seconds or minutes
   when life is just Now.

Being there, still or distracted,
   too ready sometimes
to move to the next step,
   for another short Now.

Hundred thoughts
   spinning wildly,
looking back,
   too often hurried dialogue.

Daffodil (the year 1984)

Young man bought yellow daffodil (25 cents)
        at a stand near a bookstore,
then gave the flower to the seller.
        Hours later he passed that way.
She turned to him and said
        that she was stunned for 3 minutes.

How easy to make the planet
        a happier place!

Truth in Soul

Profound notes
in intellect moving towards decision,
logic eliminating,
philosophy consoling,
theology directing.
But, on wind-swept ledge,
rising, elevating, tempting, stretching
on cultivated mountain top,
obscuring, standing sentinel, looming in
quaint meadow,
blooming, inviting blossoms to speak
in fertile valley,
enduring rocks seemingly
planted firm.
In amazing dreams looking to Now,
using scenes, figures, images saying so much
with little,
trusting increasing unconscious flow happily,
frequently hard recalling, yet so vital reaching
inwardly,
sensing persistence's rich reward.
In serene meditation striking deep,
pulsating in mind and heart,
spiritual center speaking to feet
and finger tips,
touching depth of soul,
truth therein.

III

Courage III

Life, made up of stories,
       in them what might
in love voice
       and in courage.

Alan McCoy O.F.M.

Old Soul (wisdom beyond his years)
    accepted where he was,
saw difficulties as ways to deeper understanding,
    upward path to help others.
Sadness for so much indifference
    to plight of common person.
Spoke to uneducated and educated in language
    they both could take in easily.
Used power with spiritual excellence,
    considered, decided, pushed away, no worry.
Meetings representing USA/Canada/Mexico OFMs
    in Rome,
    when asked, "Have a meeting in the east."
Consistently when he came back from Rome,
    gifts for elderly poor in appalling poverty area
    of town.
He did this for a good number of years,
    and did not spread it about.

In another vein,
      when asked if certain individuals were great,
      he smilingly replied, "You hate to count anyone out."
Felt deeply about a good day's work,
      seldom day off, rare vacation
      (his 25th anniversary a friend recalls),
real, profound sense of
      responsibility for time given.
Promoted many projects, but never himself.
      Did not write, because research and writing
would take time away from doing for others,
      just wanted to help those who entered his life.
Unquestionable virtues: poverty, prayer, humility,
      goodness, kindness, truth, generosity,
      especially compassion.
Didn't accumulate, possessed little,
      extraordinary prayer life.
St. Francis in the beginning, St. Francis in the end.

How to be Old

Did they then? Do they now?
Do they look inside at the inner child
who searches for possibilities,
and finds when he doesn't search
creativity which surfaces, and gives child within
an enjoyable ride of special delight?
Being old is about today,
this moment, nature's truth, personal
meditation strengthening the day,
solacing child's loving soul, knowing
"The child is the father of the man."
(Wordsworth 1770-1850)

Who?

Who thinks they've done enough
  in their planet walk?
No one says "Yes,"
  just better next time,
maybe to be more aware
  of systems twisting,
sidewalk absurdities,
  dream flowers without enough light,
parental love and its beauty,
  and find more frequently
the right people to be around.

Lost Time

How to feel about lost time,
        those spaces, years
about which one wonders?
        Maybe the grunt work
helped someone,
        added a stitch or two
to worn garments, and
        a bit of gentleness
to the soul of the hand that gave,
        to prioritize,
not being in the present is lost time.

Four Virtues

The four virtues I work on:
       compassion,
courage,
       kindness,
being alive to small joys.

The Way of Many

So much film over wayfarer's eyes,
        precious dollar, active power, recognized status,
misty veil covering
        beautiful bundles of possibilities.

Glancing interest in little child on 3 wheel bike,
        not elder with cane and tired look,
bread-winning woman struggling up hill after day's labor,
        senior without title or solid means.

Nor poor in dusty studios, bathroom down the hall,
        not even known to nearby neighbors,
nor the manager who collects the rent,
        like so many, they did the best they could.

How Many?

How many
    really take in dawn's special spirit,
        let in the magic of light rain,
    watch leaves create earth art,
        feel a tree's wondrous presence,

    see beauty in stream meeting ocean,
        sense mysterious secret of quiet forest,
    value overawing mountain,
        plant oak seed for great grandchildren's eyes?

Tree Memory

Never hurt anyone or anything,
      especially a tree,
it breathes you know,
      listens, sees a lot,
remembers,
      stories in rings,
cultivates imaginations,
      displays calm,
awakens art.

Small Percentage

So few,
        concern for those alone
in small room,
        lacking family,
sense of belonging,
        having enough,
someone with whom to talk
        at 9:30 p.m.,
isolated soul,
        nothing to look forward to,
no feeling of being loved deeply…
        small percentage
see through curtain
        to those without.

May they be blessed!

Thoughts for Now

How many feel
       too much failure in the story,
not enough freedom
       in the steps?
Calendars come,
       friends go,
nature there,
       deep love rare.
Science of the heavens,
       mysteries a ton,
looking down on wounded spirits
       trekking in the sun.
Still learning to be alone,
       an art, like all virtues,
getting to sense more value
       in inner space yet to be explored.
Grateful for little things so big,
       caring connections, healthy ways,
and one of the challenging hopes,
       to see the nugget in the situation.

Sugar

Skeletal children,
       starving cattle
in far-off land,
       while
I have trouble
       cutting back
on sugar.

The Challenge

At times selfish lining, unselfish core,
spirit means well, soul wants more.

Be patient with unchanging star;
accept where you are.

Deny worry's reach;
feel each day's teach.

Strive for noblest art,
wise actions from engaging heart.

Success, hopefully balancing part of life trail,
not think too much of miserable fail.

Avoid retired life on narrow shelf;
attempt repeatedly to father self.

Empathy

So much indifference to plight of common person,
      an untold number of wandering spirits
fail to feel with what others are going through,
      not picturing great souls
      in dusty, lonely studios above storefronts,
strong largeness in frail elder,
      dignity in old clothes with aimless threads,
living alone in the slums with no emotional support,
      bathroom down the hall, noise on doorstep,

another's mortgage challenge,
      renter's rising rent
and the next one sure to come,
      understandably noble minds to focus on
family needs, personal necessities, vital concerns,

      but when the advancing age of seeing comes,
and they gaze at a lot for the first time,
      will a good many consider that some have an
intuitive feeling, that a bit more of an ascetic life
      can increase awareness.

Hope on the Hard Side

"It's a hard life," she said,
>   still, a rainbow on iron-grilled window.
"Look at everything from the most favorable sense,"
>   revealed the wise teacher.
"Walk with heart,"
>   say "Thank you every day."
Everything political, of course,
>   long time to feel its firm grip,
body wears in desert sun,
>   just believe calm wells do spring up.
Woman of 80 notes,
>   "Have to look forward,"
figuring out how to get the most
>   out of each day.

Those Who Lived Over 100

Two Obituaries

1

The 109 year old man said
       the secret of his longevity,
"I never got in a hurry."

2

She died in her sleep at 114,
       lived in the Now,
didn't think of dying,
       looked at dawn with gratitude,
at light with wonder.

Didn't Realize

So many jealousies.
      Didn't realize.
Cream usually resides not that high.
      Didn't realize.
So few deep relationships.
      Didn't realize.
True love grows at its own pace.
      Didn't realize.
Pre-cognition's amazing power.
      Didn't realize.
What said to self at the core
      "runs into reality."
      Didn't realize.

Mythology

Zeus, god of sky,
>when he saw a cloud move, did he wonder why.

Ceta, goddess of sea,
>what did she think of rock and tree.

Apollo, god of art,
>now and then was his a lonely heart.

Attis, vegetarian god, truly quite a feat,
>did he EVER eat meat.

Aphrodite, goddess of love,
>was she laid back, or did she need a shove.

Demeter, goddess of harvest, growing, grain,
>did she always reign on the plain in the rain.

Wonders of wonders delight the mind,
>what truths therein to find.

Was the city of Troy conquered by a horse made of wood;
>would it do it if it could.

Did stones of Troy turn to sand,
>if so who gave the grand command.

Were the gods jealous of Jupiter's rule;
>did they think at times his ways "not cool."

Did Phoenix bird alway rise from ash;
>did it prefer recognition or cold, hard cash.

Was arrow shot at Achille's heel,
>interesting fable or was it real.

Was Roman god Hercules that strong;
>was he always right, or rarely wrong.

Were these tales truly told,
>or just surprising and quite bold.

IV

Courage IV

Time, flicker in the sky,
    may we have the wise courage
to do what we can
    for those who enter our lives.

A Prayer

To be accident, victim free,
        self, cabin, whatever in,
grateful for luck,
        ancestors wedging.

Dancing feet not to slip,
        moving shoes not to catch,
attentive ears...fresh sounds,
        able eyes...instructive sights,

energetic frame,
        sound, capable, cheerful,
docile mind picturing soft stillness,
        stimulated hope
with yesterday's rain,
        today's thunder,
tomorrow's clouds.

For dawn's silent joys,
        personal stretching,
listening prayer,
        breath, body exercise,
friends, unselfish, loyal,
        finance, enough tucked away,
amid nature's reaching voice,
        trees which reach wistfully,
waves that roar, birds that soar,
        walking trails, sheeted waterfalls,
and other spiritual sights for a kind
        soul awakening in vitalizing air.

Appreciate flowing light,
        discharge day's tasks
with honor, discernment, safety,
        handling darkening thoughts that
swirl up,
        burdening feeling which runs high.

Live conscious,
        be awake, keenly aware,
wise, shrewd, stay alert,
        know intuitively
you will leap today's and tomorrow's hurdle
        as you have done before.

In the finale, accept where I am,
        have hope for those I love,
fcel in some way I've become
        the best possible person
I can become,
        give way quickly and close,
with love a touch away.

Cherishing Mother

Mother, my love extends to touch
      the drinking glass your fingers pressed,
to remind myself of your breathing goodness,
      your strength of spirit, beauty of soul,
You will always be Spring,
      fresh, cheerful, optimistic,
looking at the bright side,
      even in chilling rain.
You have spoken with love,
      shown boundless caring,
deeper than the ocean,
      higher than the sky.
You believed in me when
      I didn't believe in myself.
My memory and life will always be engraved
      with your love.

Words

"Talk less, say more."*

How so?

Believe in you,

feel deep,

and your words will come

with a touch of new.

Swedish Proverb

At 100

At 100,
      don't want a party,
with candles and decorated cake,
      a comic, smiling song,
as if to say "Soon you'll be gone."
      Just a few a touch away
who **heard** me along the way.

Another Day II

Daily challenge,
accept what is,
avoid the toxic,
deal with what you can control,
when dark dwelling comes,
      stays too long, try to be strong and move along,
find activities which distract,
go one's course on what gives hope.

Olden Days

He appreciates looking back,
    living on a block
from which one does not stray,
    churches open during the day,
community support
    fostering safety and a good feeling,
pride of workmanship,
    particular manners,
neighborhood helping, kind,
    less money, more renters,
fewer autos, more public transportation,
    harmonious unity in traditions,
often temple as a guiding star,
    gentle comfort
from old-fashioned flat
    on Hartford Street
that was Home,
    a simple life,
beans on payday.
    He remembers
saying to his mother,
    "We're poor,"
she responding,
    "We are not poor;
we are Lower Middle Class."

Those were the happiest days.

Mi Casa

Would that I had a property by ocean shore,
   to build a house that would be "Me,"
kitchen, creative and large,
   bedrooms, charming, waving waters in sight,
wide-walled, artistic pictures hanging fondly,
   new wood, fresh aroma in the air,
there to create word dreams,
   allowing pen to reach pinnacle heights,
art on moonlit nights,
   overriding hundreds of thoughts
trying to labor in manifold distractions,
   windows providing splendid view,
to gaze out, feel nature's breath,
   discover unwritten messages
from the sea.

Elder Time

People have virtue, do more good than they realize,
          yet when one is sick or quite poor, friends defined,
life's way, many human souls have difficulty responding.

Still, celebrate season's new beginning,
          another spiritual opportunity, time teaching,
so big, belief, attitude, wholeness in the moment.

The Mind and the Years

The mind sails into varied waters,
     new wind, tossing tide,
still, ever awake
     to something mighty;
wonders about trail ahead
     cloaked in unexplored mystery,
perhaps slides, rocks, stones on pragmatic path,
     where sense and luck a buoyant hope,
to relish little joys,
     prize fresh rose,
calm bird resting on thin branch,
     serious art speaking to the soul.

Getting Older

Older folks feel losses
        they never thought they would,
nor anticipate they'd be there
        in that reality…
at what age,
        when friends withdraw,
people who hear them thin,
        wonder why they connected with so few.

Advantages though,
        twilight courage,
living the virtues, forgiving enemies,
        extra careful…
feel love's value
        like never before,
focus on what they can control,
        prioritize what to get done,
ask self,
        what means most?

Worry

At times everyone's companion,
        to deny its effects,
push to table edge,
        perhaps breathe two minutes,
then on with the day,
        do the enjoyable,
going forward wisely,
        try to balance
vigilance, serenity,
        and trust.

Right Questions

Why have I not asked the right questions often?
  I think of them later,
when you can't go back and say, "By the way,"
  sadly, smart too late.
It was the best I could do at the time.
  What can I do now?
Nurture self with compassion.
  Be conscious of the strength of vigilance.

There All the Time

To go down to the creek
     and forget the world,
imagine
     magic fish jumping out of water,
joyful birds swooping down eyeing their leap,
     tame deer stopping to drink, talking to me,
no weather annoyance
     nor discord in the day,
then finding sacred art
     carved in time-worn stone,
there all the time.

Ode to an Acquaintance

You are unique in all the world,
        but isn't everyone.
You try to become friends with people,
        an error, of course,
friendship either happens or it doesn't,
        so do not say
"I want to be your friend."
        You think you are prayerful. You are!
But if it takes 40 years to learn how to study
        (and it does),
how long does it take to learn how to pray?
        You call yourself busy. Not a falsehood.
In life's whole span, how many organize
        time with consistency?
You are politically non-political at 28…29.
        How will you maneuver at 40…41?
You see alternatives on heartfelt paths. Good!
        Something to develop and control.
You are a child of the '60s and '70s.
        However the greatest time is before us.
May you listen to its feelings, its thoughts,
        and what the world does not say!

Threads

Friend-threads, sometimes
    thinner with time,
great love just gets better,
    love loss, tragedy at evening-tide.

Courage-threads, sometimes
    stronger with time,
great courage just gets greater,
    courage loss, tragedy at evening-tide.

Creativity-threads, sometimes
    come in waves,
great creativity reward of genes and hard work,
    creativity loss, tragedy at evening-tide.

Heart of a Child Again

Reaching an age of reason,
    the mind says
"I'll never be a child again."

Still, chaste-like hand
    able to produce great art,
so too, loving eyes that smile and dance.

Though life ushers in age,
    rare spirit can have
heart of a child again.

Two Birds

Appraising eyes
      turning its head from the others,
perhaps indicating a mind of its own,
      away from the crowd,
but with strength to fly on,
      singing its own song.

Another bird
      chirps contentedly,
seemingly comfortable where it is.

80 Years

We belong to time,*
       place too,
sacred spirits
       having a human experience.

To manage,
       think differently,
stay present,
       focus on purposes.

At 10, everything important,
       25, priorities take hold,
80, health, love/family, money,
       yet everything is important.

Albert Camus 1913-1960

Missed Opportunities

How many have not seen shiny pebble
      on dusty path,
which would have helped anxious spirit
      skip in the rain?

Years pass, vision improves,
      "should of" comes to mind,
small voice whispers, "Had other priorities then,
      was the best human spirit could do."

Compassion

Ragged painter in the sun, with skillful brush,
　　smiling at sidewalk cracks, and mud without lotus.
An artistic life, some stimulating sentences,
　　handful of metaphors,
　　　　sacred symbols that take shape in time.
Vocal colorist, sprinkling spiritual song,
　　one of mind, spirit, and hand,
　　　　created by meditation,
　　　　lofty and serene,
　　sifted wisdom ripening wholesomely
　　　　on examining finger tips.
Realistic novelist with a mirror who forgives all,
　　even stacks of synthetic straw
　　　　leaning beneath misty, iron-grilled windows.
True poet, loving whispering trees, billowy seas,
　　who feels the wind's ringing, secret messages,
　　　　who breathes gently on time standing still,
　　allowing the unexplored mystery to unfold.

Within the dancing stream of undefinable longing.
　　may you always feel safe in the powder of God!

"To Choose One's Attitude"

Four concentration camps, World War II,
    including the infamous **Auschwitz,**
    weighty wisdom from a heroic survivor,

    "The one thing you can't take away from me is the way
    I choose to respond to what you do to me. The last of one's
    *freedoms is to **choose one's attitude** in any given circumstances."**

I as a common person have the same choice,

without the overwhelming difficulties of
    barbed wire, armed guards, staring walls,
    poor food, listless rest, lacking bread-winning work,
    with consuming uncertainties, deadly surprises,
    powerful awareness of the day's fearful possibilities,
    hopeless, helpless feeling, harsh treatment, discarded dignity,
    rejections of thoughts of hate, cruelty of ungentle fate.

with most of us more blessed, enjoying
    wholesome diet, good water, comfortable sleep,
    safe shelter, daily shower, arbitrary exercise,
    joyful celebrations, emotional significance,
    love connection with family, warm friendships,
    easier to plant seeds, sing, walk around the block,
    and special ones now and then to say "I love you."

**Victor Frankl, 1905-1997*
Author of Man's Search for Meaning

ACKNOWLEDGEMENTS

Joan Arnott

Barbara Elenteny

Sheila Helms

Eliane McCaffrey

Rev. Bill McDonald

Nancy Ricker Rhett

MeMe Riordan

Aidan, grandson in heart, and the author

ABOUT THE AUTHOR

CHARLES HOLMES is an educated and creative soul. His perhaps most important work, *Streets That Speak*, is about streets that do not have enough and streets that do have enough. His poems in *Reflections of the Heart*, *Reflections of the Soul*, and *For Understanding Eyes* offer meditative moments for quiet consideration. His interviews in *Thoughts From Millie* are a collection of rich common sense from an elder when she was 89, 90, and 91 years of age.

He is a surrogate grandfather to a 10 year old boy named Aidan.

He has delved into the magic of study formally and privately for many years.

He has created three recreation centers for children, has taught at two universities and one community college, has done social work with the elderly poor, and has authored two studies about their difficulties.

He also has written eight children's books (page v). Some are fun; others, sort of "cool." Still others are on the serious side.

He hopes that *Reflections of the Soul* conveys to the reader a feeling, as well as a thought or two.

To contact the author,
please email
rlg121212@gmail.com

53905189R00052

Made in the
USA
Lexington, KY